Precision Rifle Range Book

By

Paul G. Markel

Precision Rifle Range Book

Paul G. Markel

Copr. 2022

All Rights Reserved

Cover Design: Zachary J. Markel

Shooter's Info

This rifle range book is the property of:

____

Rifle
Manufacturer: _______________________________
Model:_____________________

Caliber:_____________________
Serial Number: _____________________

Optic
Manufacturer:_______________________
Model:_______________________

BZO: _______________
Elevation: _______________

Ammunition

Manufacturer:_______________________________

Bullet Weight:_______________________
Velocity:_______________

Foreword

In 1987 I became a United States Marine. One of the many benefits of membership in the world's largest fraternity is the education in rifle marksmanship that every Marine receives at basic training. For two solid weeks, the foundational principles of marksmanship were not just drilled into our heads, they were practiced for hours on end during dry-fire sessions that we called "Grass Week".

By the time we were issued our first pieces of live ammunition to BZO (battle-sight zero) our M16A2 rifles, each of us had already taken over a thousand deliberate trigger presses. Consider that for a moment. How many contemporary shooters have the mental discipline to put in that kind of effort? How many would even conduct 100 perfect trigger presses, much less 1000 before dropping the firing pin on a live round?

It might be easy to say, "Well, that's the Marine Corps. Not everyone is a Marine." While that is a true statement, what we were taught on Parris Island was not a closely guarded state secret. We didn't take a blood oath promising to take that confidential information to the grave.

I had a natural love for firearms and shooting and as such I soaked up every word that our Primary

Marksmanship Instructor said. I took the dry-fire seriously and tried to make every single trigger press perfect. Like myself, those others in my platoon who took Grass Week seriously and applied what we were taught scored an "Expert" rating on qualification day.

Fast forward to 1990 and all of the Expert Marksmen in my Rifle Company were sent to Marine Corps Rifle and Pistol Marksmanship Coaches School. During that two week school we focused on teaching those rifle fundamentals we all had learned in Basic Training as well as handgun marksmanship. Naturally, the primary focus was how to teach or coach our fellow Marines on the range. Again, there were no magic or top secret techniques, only a solid focus on the application of the fundamentals.

More than a decade later, I found myself in a Sniper School. Even though I was using a .308 Winchester rifle with a high-powered, adjustable scope, it was those same foundational marksmanship fundamentals that would earn me my certificate. When I made my first hit on a target at 1000 yards, and then 1400, and then 1 mile, it was the fundamentals that I used on the Parris Island Rifle Range that helped me put the bullets on steel.

I did not relate the previous to sound braggadocious or arrogant, I relate my experience to drive home the concept that, when it comes to putting a single round from a rifle on target, on demand, there is no secret formula. Expert rifle marksmanship is the product of diligent effort and the supreme mental discipline to master the fundamentals and then apply them for each and every shot, without fail.

When I teach my students, I remind them that I can explain and demonstrate everything they need to know to be an expert marksman. What I cannot do is get into their heads and make them apply what they have been taught. That, my dear reader, is where I leave it with you. This book cannot teach you to shoot a rifle, it is meant to be a tool for you, a way to remember to apply all of those fundamentals and then to track your progress.

Also, before you begin reading, I would suggest grabbing a pencil for notetaking and a highlighter.

Paul G. Markel, April 2022

Contents

Glossary of Common Marksmanship Terms

Atmospheric Mirage: this is a combination of air temperature, humidity, and sunlight that combine to obscure sight of the target.

Ballistic Coefficient: Relative to the design of the projectile, the BC affects the flight path of the projectile as it passes through the atmosphere. The higher the BC, the more efficient the flight of the projectile.

Bone Support: The use of the skeletal frame to support the rifle in various shooting positions.

BRASS-F: Acronym meaning "Breathe, Relax, Aim, Squeeze, Surprise, Follow-Through", used to remind shooter's of fundamentals.

Bullet Trace: The visible path of the projectile as it passes through the atmosphere, generally only visible through magnified optic.

Bullet Trajectory: The actual path of the projectile in flight. Bullets, like all else, are subject to the effects of gravity.

Buttstock: The rear portion of the rifle: the top of the stock is the comb, the bottom is the belly, the back end is the butt, the top of the butt is the heel and the bottom of the butt is the toe.

BZ0 (Battle-sight Zero): The zero setting on your adjustable sights expressed in distance ie: 25 meters, 100 yards, etc. Most magnified optics are BZO'd for 100 yards or meters by the shooter.

Click: A single increment of adjustment on either the elevation or windage knobs of a scope

Dominant Side/Hand: This is the side of the body that corresponds to the dominant eye. The dominant hand holds the grip and presses the trigger.

DOPE: Acronym meaning Data on Personal Equipment, translates to the elevation and windage settings on the adjustable sight. Also, has been seen as "Data of Previous Engagement"

Elevation: Adjustments for bullet strike at distances expressed in Up or Down (Not to be confused with Geographic Elevation)

Eye Relief: The distance of the shooter's eye from the rear sight or focal lens of a scope.

First Focal Plane: Scope reticle is placed forward, toward the objective lens. In a 1st Focal Plane variable power optic the reticle appears to get larger as the power is increased. This is the preferred set up for range estimating or MilDot reticles.

Focal Lens: The lens of the rifle scope nearest to the shooter's eye. Used to adjust the focus of scope to the shooter's vision.

Forend/Forearm: The forward portion of the rifle where the support hand holds the gun.

Free-floated: Refers to the barrel of a precision rifle where the barrel is secured in such a way that the stock or forend does not make contact with it.

Geographic Elevation: Not to be confused with the elevation setting on a rifle scope, geographic elevation affects the flight of the projectile. The higher the elevation, the less resistance the bullet encounters, therefore the trajectory becomes "flatter" at higher elevations.

Harmonics: During the fraction of a second when the rifle discharges and the projectile passes through the bore, the barrel will flex.

Hold Over: Technique used by the spotter to aid the shooter in making a rapid follow up shot after the first shot has missed the mark. Expressed in various ways, ie: inches, MILS, etc.

MilDot Reticle: Scope reticle expressed in MILS, distance between each dot is 1 MIL. Used for range estimation and hold over.

Milliradian: Also MRAD or MILS, scope adjustments expressed in tenths on the elevation and windage knobs of a rifle scope. 1 MIL is equal to 10 'click' adjustments of the knob. 1 full MIL is equal to 10 centimeters of adjustment at 100 yards or 3.6 inches

MOA: Minute of Angle, expressed as 1 inch of adjustment per 100 yards, adjustments for both the elevation and windage knobs on a rifle scope. Adjustments may be ¼, ⅓ ½, or 1 MOA depending on the make and model of optic.

Natural Point of Aim: The relation of the shooter and rifle to the target which requires the least amount of muscle tension to maintain.

Natural Respiratory Pause: The moment between when the shooter inhales and then exhales a breath from their lungs.

Objective Lens: The lens of the rifle scope farthest from the shooter's eye. Expressed in millimeters, ie: "50mm Lens" etc. Generally speaking, the larger the objective lens the better the light gathering capability of the optic.

Parallax Knob: Also referred to as a "focus knob", used to clarify scope focus for various targets distances and environmental conditions.

Reticle: Aiming device within rifle scope, varies tremendously depending on manufacturer.

Second Focal Plane: Scope reticle is placed rearward toward the focal lens. In a variable power optic, the reticle size appears constant, regardless of the power setting.

Spotter: Shooting partner who observes bullet impact to assist the shooter.

Spotting Scope: A stand alone optic, not mounted to a rifle, used by a spotter to witness the impact of the shooter's shot.

Stock Weld: Also referred to as cheek weld, refers to the exact placement of the shooter's cheek onto the rifle stock.

Support Side/Hand: This side is the opposite of the dominant one. The support side hand and arm "supports" or holds up the front end of the rifle.

Tube: Main body of scope expressed in size: 1 inch, 30mm, 34mm, etc. used to determine light transmission, scope ring size, and amount of adjustment in target knobs.

Windage: Adjustments for bullet strike on the horizontal plane expressed in Left or Right

The author (center bald man) being promoted to Lance Corporal in a galaxy far, far away.

USMC Rifleman's Creed

Major General William H. Rupertus, USMC

1. This is my rifle. There are many like it, but this one is mine.

2. My rifle is my best friend. It is my life. I must master it as I must master my life.

3. My rifle, without me, is useless. Without my rifle, I am useless. I must fire my rifle true. I must shoot straighter than my enemy who is trying to kill me. I must shoot him before he shoots me. I will …

4. My rifle and myself know that what counts in this war is not the rounds we fire, the noise of our burst, nor the smoke we make. We know that it is the hits that count. We will hit….

5. My rifle is human, even as I, because it is my life. Thus, I will learn it as a brother. I will learn its weaknesses, its strength, its parts, its accessories, its sights and its barrel. I will ever guard it against the ravages of weather and damage as I will ever guard my legs, my arms, my eyes and my heart against damage. I will keep my rifle clean and ready. We will become part of each other. We will ….

6. Before God, I swear this creed. My rifle and myself are the defenders of my country. We are the

masters of our enemy. We are the saviors of my life.

7. So be it, until victory is America's and there is no enemy, but peace!!

The Author training in Wyoming winter.

Chapter 1

Foundational Marksmanship Principles for Rifles

Going back to my time on the Parris Island Rifle Range during the summer of 1987, please allow me to relate the foundational marksmanship principles for rifle shooting that I was taught.

The tool we were using at that time was the M16A2 rifle, an upgraded version of the M16A1 with certain features that made it a better tool for precision or distance shooting.

As an aside, the rate of twist on the A2 was changed to 1-in-7 from the 1-in-12 of the A1. This allowed for greater stability of heavier projectiles. The length of the stock was increased an inch from the A1 and the barrel was a bit heavier.

Also, the sights on the M16A2 were improved. On the original M16A1 sights the elevation was adjusted up front and windage in the rear, the A2 rear sight was modified to allow it to be adjusted for both windage and elevation after the front sight was adjusted for BZO.

One of the first things our PMI taught us was how to take our standard rifle sling and make it into a loop sling to be used for rock solid stability. That skill is a bit of a lost art form today. Regardless of position; we shot from prone, sitting, kneeling, and standing (off-hand), two principles were important; bone support and natural point of aim.

Bone support is understanding how to support your shooting position using your skeletal frame, not your muscles. The way it was explained to me three plus decades ago was, "Muscles get tired and start to shake, bones don't get tired."

Natural point of aim is the process of aligning your body and rifle in such a way that the muzzle of your gun is naturally pointing at the target. We test natural point of aim by getting into our shooting position and aiming at the target. Next, we close our eyes, inhale deeply and exhale, then open our eyes. Is the rifle still on target or has it shifted? If the rifle is still indexed on target, you have a natural point of aim. If not, you need to adjust your position and try again.

If you are muscling your rifle into position, it is possible to make a good shot. However, a second or third shot is going to become more difficult as your muscles tire and begin to tremble. By using bone support and natural point of aim, you can consistently place shot after shot on target without experiencing physical fatigue. Additionally, the shooter can remain in position while waiting for an opportunity to take a shot for much longer if they practice good bone support.

The conundrum of making a precise shot with a rifle is that you must hold the gun as perfectly still as possible, while at the same time applying muscle tension/pressure to the trigger to release the firing pin. Also, in the real world, the rifle is being held in the hands of a living creature, not secured in a bench vice.

Living humans have to breathe and their heart is always beating. Muscles tense and then relax. All of this can translate to movement in the rifle at the moment of ignition. Too much movement and the shot will miss.

By using bone support and natural point of aim, we hope to reduce the amount of muscle tension and movement to an absolute minimum. The only perceptible muscle movement you want is the tension in your trigger finger.

BRASS-F

After we were taught the correct ways to use bone support in the prone, sitting, kneeling and off-hand, our PMI introduced us to a shooter's mantra called BRASS-F. Allow me to dissect each part of this acronym.

Breathe - We all need to breathe, but a rifleman must control his breathing. We control our breathing and make it slow and steady. Holding your breath will cause your body to crave oxygen and the tremors will come quickly. Ditto for breathing out completely. Instead we steady our breathing and learn to press the trigger during the natural respiratory pause.

When breathing normally, there is a natural pause of about 3 to 4 seconds between when you inhale and then exhale. It is during this pause that we complete the trigger press and fire the shot.

Relax - By relax we mean check your body for muscle tension and ensure we are using bone support. To make a consistently perfect shot, your body should be as free of muscle tension as possible. Often, shooters will find that they have muscle tension in their shoulders and neck area. That tension will screw up the shot.

Aim - This is when we ensure that our sights are indexed on the target correctly and that we are ready for the trigger to release. Your visual focus needs to be on the front sight or maintaining the reticle in position.

Squeeze - Yes, the accepted term is "press" the trigger, not squeeze, but P doesn't work in the acronym. Squeeze simply means begin to apply steady, deliberate pressure to the trigger until it releases. We use the pad (fingerprint area) of our trigger finger to press the trigger straight back towards our body.

Surprise - The ignition of the shot should provide a slight surprise. This is where we lose a lot of people. "I'm pressing the trigger so I know the gun will go off. I'm not going to be surprised."

The surprise part of BRASS-F is included to help eliminate that natural human desire to anticipate the shot/recoil. When your finger begins to press the trigger your mind should not be on the rifle firing. Your mind and focus should be holding the rifle/sights perfectly still on the target.

Follow-Through - Follow-Through means to ride the recoil of the rifle and come back down behind the sights on target. On the training range, follow through helps to avoid the tendency to flinch or recoil anticipation. In the field, follow through puts you back on target so you know whether or not a second shot is required.

I have been using BRASS-F for well over thirty years now. I have applied BRASS-F for .22LR rifles all the way up to the Barrett M82A1 .50 BMG. If you don't think you will ever flinch, try shooting a shoulder fired .50 BMG or magnum calibers such as the .300 Winchester Magnum or .338 Lapua Magnum.

I tell my students that I teach them BRASS-F so that they can some day forget it. If you apply this basic marksmanship mantra in a disciplined manner for long enough, it will eventually become a natural and subconscious part of your shooting routine. You will just do it without having to think about it. We call this unconscious competence.

Chapter 2   Consistency

Another fundamental of marksmanship is one that cannot be taught but it must be applied by every shooter and that is consistency.

Consistency is what we call "The Big C" in marksmanship. Anyone can hit the center of the target accidentally or once in a while if they launch enough bullets. Our goal is to be able to hit the target each and every time, on demand whenever we get behind our rifle.

There are some tips for consistency. We have already discussed bone support, natural point of aim and BRASS-F.

To be consistent with our rifle, you need to hold it and position your body on it the same way. Stock weld and eye relief go hand in hand. Stock weld is also referred to as "cheek weld" and that is the position and manner your cheek is placed on the comb of the rifle stock. Generally speaking, you want your cheek bone to touch the comb of the stock in the same place. Some competition shooters go so far as to place a piece of tape in the stock exactly where their cheek should touch it. Your stock weld will be determined by your eye relief, the distance that your shooting eye is from the rear sight or the focal lens of the scope.

After you have taken the time to fine tune the focal lens to your vision, you should see down the rifle scope in a perfect circle. If there is shadow in the scope picture right, left, up or down, you need to adjust the placement of your cheek on the stock. Adjustable rifle stocks were designed to allow the shooter to get as perfect of a stock weld and eye relief as possible. *Remember, creeping up on the scope of a powerful, centerfire rifle can be a painful and bloody experience.*

The stock weld also includes how you place the butt of the rifle stock into the socket of your shoulder. The stock should not be on your collar bone, nor should it be so far out that it touches where your upper arm and shoulder meet.

A good stock weld and eye relief should be accomplished without muscle strain in your neck or shoulders. If your neck muscles begin to ache while you are in position, you need to make a correction.

Another form of consistency is how you place your shooting hand on the grip portion of the rifle. The grip will vary tremendously depending on the rifle design. Regardless, you want a natural, relaxed grip with our shooting hand. The rifle should be supported by your forward/support hand and your shoulder. You should be able to take your shooting hand off of the rifle and have it stay in place.

As touched on earlier, the portion of your finger that makes contact with the flat surface of the trigger should be the pad, the finger print area. One cue that I give my students is to tell them that I should be able to use my Detective Kit and pull a perfect finger print off of their trigger face.

When it comes time to take the shot, the finger should apply steady direct pressure rearward. This is where muscle tension is being applied to the rifle. A straight rearward press should not disturb your sight picture. A disturbed sight picture generally cannot be perceived with iron sights, but with a high powered rifle scope this disturbance is perceptible.

Thanks to modern engineering, the triggers on rifles today are lightyears ahead of where they were when I was lying in the grass on Parris Island. For a precision rifle, the trigger weight should be around 3.5 to 4 pounds. Lighter triggers lead to "oops" moments. Also, if a trigger is tuned too lightly, light primer strikes can become an issue. There is absolutely no reason a trained rifleman cannot easily manage a 4 pound trigger. The triggers on our M16A2 rifles hovered in the 8 pound range and we were still able to hit human silhouettes at 500 yards with iron sights. People who blame the trigger on their rifle need more training.

As mentioned earlier, an instructor cannot *teach* you consistency. The instructor can teach you how to get into position, hold the rifle, and work the machine, but consistency comes from mental discipline. It is the responsibility of the shooter to apply all they have been taught, not just occasionally, but for each and every shot.

The instructor cannot get into the shooter's head and make them run through BRASS-F for each shot. That is the responsibility of the man behind the rifle. Those who are able to embrace mental and physical discipline are those who will be able to achieve expert marksman status.

Consistent accuracy comes from dedication.

Consistency in Equipment

Another part of consistency is the consistency of equipment. If you want to learn how to shoot a rifle exceedingly well, you need to pick one rifle/scope/ammunition combination and stick with it.

Far too many American men suffer from "Newgearitis". These folks are constantly looking for the new and improved. They barely have their first gun broken in and they are looking for the newest, coolest, hottest thing. I've known guys who had barely put fifty rounds through a gun, but they had to trade it to get whatever was on the cover of the latest gun magazine.

Sure, the rifling in a barrel can wear out, but you need to actually shoot the gun for that to happen. Modern factory firearms are put together on an assembly line. Most of them actually shoot better and run more smoothly after fifty to a hundred rounds or more. This does not apply to a custom build, but even a custom rifle barrel needs to be shot to tighten up.

Ammunition choice is another way to tell the professionals from the amateurs. If you need or desire to do high volume shooting with your AR or AK, sure buy inexpensive training ammo. However, when it comes to making one perfect shot after another, ammunition choice is paramount.

Regardless of caliber, all rifles tend to favor certain loads over others. I have been testing and evaluating rifles for thirty years. Even custom precision rifles that will shoot every round sub-MOA will favor certain loads over others. This has much to do with the rifling of the barrel, but there are other less obvious factors as well.

As a general rule, heavier/longer bullets perform better with a faster rate of twist. Conversely, lighter, faster moving projectiles will perform with a slower twist rate.

With all that said, the best way to determine which loads function and pattern the most consistently in your rifle is to test it. My standard practice with a new rifle is to secure at least three different loads of that caliber (boxes of 20 will suffice). I block out some time where I will not be rushed and enjoy the shooting experience.

For instance, if I have a new .308 Winchester bolt-action rifle I might bring out a box of 155 grain, a 168 grain and 175 grain ammunition. After taking my time and patterning these three loads I will have a definite feeling for which one is more consistent in that rifle.

If you are very serious, you can take the winner of the three, let's say it was 175 and then try different 175 grain loads of various bullet designs and velocities. Soon you will discover exactly which load your rifle prefers. With that information in hand, dedicate that load for that rifle and you should be on your way.

Chapter 3

One Shot is All that Matters

In our world of standard capacity rifle magazines that hold thirty rounds, it is easy to slip into the mental laziness of thinking, *"I have 30 rounds, it doesn't matter if the first couple miss."* Such is not the thinking of a true rifleman.

When I set foot on the property occupied by the Weapons Training Battalion on Parris Island I read the red sign with yellow/gold lettering that stated; "We train the world's finest marksmen." I had no idea on that first day what I was about to experience.

In 1987, the standard capacity magazine for the M16A2 rifle held thirty rounds. I was a bit surprised that, when we began our live fire portion of training, we were issued wooden loading blocks to stage our rounds. We were instructed to feed each round into our rifles singly, that is, one at a time for slow fire. Yes, there were rapid fire stages where we fired 5 rounds, swapped magazines and fired 5 more. However, for the 200, 300, and 500 yard slow fire stages, only one round was loaded at a time.

When you are a recruit you do not ask questions, but I wondered why we did not simply load the number of rounds required for the slow fire stage.

It was not until I had more experience that I understood the genius of this training technique. By requiring us to load only a single round into our rifles, our instructors were forcing us to put our entire mental focus on making one hit with one round. We did not have "extra" shots to try and figure it out. Every round we fired was *the round.* That was just one of the many ways that mental discipline was instilled in us.

Go back to the Rifleman's Creed referenced earlier.

My rifle and myself know that what counts in this war is not the rounds we fire, the noise of our burst, nor the smoke we make. We know that it is the hits that count. We will hit....

Major General Rupertus understood what it meant to be a true rifleman, to be an expert marksman. Any retard can grab a rifle and yank on the trigger until it stops making noise. But, the man who can deliberately place every round in that magazine on target is one to be feared and respected.

Many years after Basic Training and Coaches School I would find myself working with seasoned veterans from all of the Armed Forces of the United States. I had assumed that each service provided solid, fundamental marksmanship training to its members. I was sadly mistaken. I had one Navy Seal remark about the load one/fire one training,

"That is stupid. The mag holds thirty. Put 28 in it and run the gun as it was intended." Back then we were operating under the *"Never load more than 28 rounds in an M16 magazine"* policy.

Most of my comrades from the Army, Navy, and Air Force could not fathom the wisdom of disciplining a shooter to focus on each and every shot. When I discussed the BRASS-F mantra, I was told that the *surprise* part was "stupid" or "pointless", because all of the shooters knew the rifle would recoil and make noise when the trigger was pulled.

This, ladies and gentleman, is the difference between someone who learns to be *good* with a rifle and someone who trains to become *great* with one. As I mentioned at the very beginning of this book, none of the fundamentals of rifle marksmanship are high level secrets or magic. The path toward becoming an expert rifleman is taken one shot at a time.

Some readers might be thinking, "Well, the military has an unlimited supply of ammunition. Anyone can become an expert if they are given thousands of rounds."

The men in my Boot Camp platoon and I, who went from never having fired an M16A2 rifle to qualifying as Experts two weeks later, fired no more than 250 rounds total. It is not the volume of ammunition that matters, it is what you do with each and every round you have.

We train to make every shot the best shot

Chapter 4

Cold Shots and Calling your Shots

The "cold shot" is the shot that is made without warming up, that is, the first shot through the barrel. From a mechanical or scientific standpoint, the first shot through a cold or air temperature barrel will impact just a bit differently than successive shots through a warm or hot barrel.

The steel of your rifle barrel will relax or expand ever so slightly as it heats up. This affects the friction of the projectile as it passes along the lands and grooves of the bore. Naturally, heavy/match barrels take longer to heat up than do lightweight or field barrels.

The barrel on a hunting rifle will naturally be lighter or thinner than that of a match or precision rifle. A hunter wants to reduce the rifle weight because he is hiking and climbing. The first shot from a hunter's rifle is the most important one. Most wild game won't stand around to let you warm up and eventually get a hit on target.

Long range, sniper, and/or match rifles have heavy barrels because these take much longer to heat up to the point where accuracy is affected. The trade off is that the rifle weighs much more than a field/hunting gun. Most match shooters only carry their rifles from the truck to the firing line and back again. Law enforcement sharpshooters have a bit farther to go but they don't generally hump for miles with their rifles. The military sniper has a heavy rifle and they simply must have the muscle to go with it.

Cold shots, however, are not just about temperature. The cold shot is the shooter's first shot of the day, the week, the hunt, the mission, whatever. This is where all of the fundamentals come back to us.

For a shooter at a match, the first shot of the day can and will often set the tone for the competition. If the first shot is an "X", the shooter's confidence is bolstered and the brain is flooded with the good chemicals. However, if the first shot of the match is a poor shot, now the shooter must mentally fight to shake that off and move on.

A missed first shot for a hunter often means that a trophy animal just took off and is gone for the day or forever. Again, we are dealing with a crushing mental feeling.

For the law enforcement or military sniper, a missed first shot could mean that a bad person will continue to do bad things and good people will be hurt or killed. You might get him with shot number two, but how much damage did he do in the meantime?

After you have had proper training and understand how and what to practice, the best way to approach the first shot of a training or practice session is to focus on that first, cold shot. We are back to the idea of discipline. You must discipline yourself to make the first shot of the day the best or the most perfect shot.

The undisciplined amatuer has the mindset that they need to warm-up and take some practice shots first before they can be expected to make a good shot. Conversely, the disciplined professional understands that excuses are Toro Caca and that they can and will make the first shot count.

Calling your Shots

Going back to the Parris Island Rifle Range, we were issued an M16 Data Book to use to record each and every shot we fired. There were little target images in our books that mimicked those that we were shooting. Our instructor taught us to "call" that shot after we completed the follow-through.

"I want you to be honest and ask yourself, how did the shot feel?" our instructor admonished us. "Did you anticipate the recoil?" or "Did you lose focus of the front sight before the shot broke?" Calling your shot was meant to teach us to self-evaluate our performance and use that evaluation to make corrections. If we make a bad shot, our coach would ask us, "Did you call the shot? What went wrong?"

A few years later, I took a professional photography class using 35mm SLR cameras and film. During the class our instructor admonished us that with experience and practice, we would get a feeling or "know" when the shutter snapped whether it was going to be a good shot or not. As I progressed in my photographic endeavors, I was able to achieve that goal. Before the advent of digital cameras, when the shutter snapped, I would know if the picture would be a good one

With training and experience, a rifleman will learn that same trick. The moment the shot breaks you should know whether it was a good one. Yes, if you are taking a shot at an unknown distance, you might need to add some elevation, but that is just math. If you miss a target, you must be able to call your shot and understand whether the miss was the fault of the shooter or simply the need for a dope adjustment.

Shooters with an inability to call their shots will spend ridiculous amounts of time chasing hits. They miss the target and immediately adjust their dope. Then they miss again and make another adjustment and so it goes. Before you touch your target knobs, you must be honest with yourself. If you lost focus at the last second, admit it to yourself and try again. Everyone makes a bad shot once in a while, that's not a sin. The only sin is to fail to learn from it.

I was once at the rifle range of a shooting club and the guy on the bench next to me said that he put a new scope on his rifle and needed to zero it. I went about my business, but I noticed that after every shot, the gentleman would reach up and adjust the elevation or the windage. An hour later, I packed up my things to leave and he was still trying to zero his scope at 100 yards.

*Author's Note: Some of you might be thinking *"You are an instructor, why didn't you help the guy out?"* I learned long ago, whether in the gym or at the range, I do not give unsolicited advice. Ninety-nine times out of one hundred, the party in need of advice will either dismiss it out of hand or simply say "Thanks, I've got it."

Chapter 5

Shooting Positions

There is an epidemic in the community of the modern rifle shooter. This sickness is actually an addiction. This addition is to the shooting bench.

Thanks to the convenience of shooting clubs and public ranges, modern rifle shooters have become accustomed to having a solid shooting bench from which to launch projectiles from their rifles.

Don't get me wrong, having a solid shooting bench is a wonderful situation when you need to to zero your rifle's sights or optic. Also, if you need to test pattern different loads, you want your rifle to be as solid and steady as possible. However, in my humble opinion, far too many folks who would be riflemen become addicted to the shooting bench and form a psychological attachment to it.

I completely understand this addiction. From the shooting bench, people discover that they can shoot nice, tight, brag-worthy shot groups. They love to pull their targets and show their tight groups to their friends. These folks like shooting the tight groups and are afraid if they get up from the bench their shot groups won't look so good.

To be fair, if shooting a rifle is your hobby and you never plan to take your gun anywhere but your local gun club, have at it. Shoot from the bench to your heart's content. Just understand that you are limiting yourself. A well-rounded, expert marksman can shoot from any number of positions whether they are supported by a bench, a bipod, a backpack or just the bones.

During our precision rifle classes, none of our shooters get to use the bench until they have proven themselves on the shooting mat and have worked through the four (4) fundamental shooting positions: prone (no rest), sitting, kneeling, and off-hand (standing).

There is a time to use the bench and a time not to.

We remind our students that there are no shooting benches out there in the real world. *(Yes, we are aware that some varmint shooters actually take portable benches to the field.)*

Four Fundamental Shooting Positions

*Editor's Note: these positions are for maximum stability and are not supposed to be "tactical".

Prone: The prone position is essentially lying on the ground. Prone is the most stable of all unsupported shooting positions because the shooter is hugging Mother Earth and gravity has only a small effect on the shooter and their rifle.

In the prone position, we want our elbows on the ground and our humerus bones (upper arms) as vertical as possible. This position minimizes the need for our arm muscles to hold our positions. If the elbows flare out or even inward, we need our muscles to hold them steady. Remember, the goal is bone support, not muscle support.

Thanks to the Little Green Army Men, American men believe that they have to draw up one of their knees and cock their legs when shooting in the prone. Such a position puts muscle tension in the legs and the lower back. This muscle tension can migrate to the upper back.

We teach our students to let their lower body go limp in the prone position. We do not cross our ankles or cock one leg up on a knee. For the prone, your legs are not required so relax them.

Prone: Note shooter's legs are flat, not cocked.

Prone (close up): Elbows are shoulder width apart in order to maintain bone support.

Sitting: Going back to Kindergarten, we are going to sit on the ground with our ankles crossed, you know "Indian style". Sitting is the next most stable position as again, gravity has a minimum effect on the shooter.

A young, limber shooter can cross their ankles and allow their legs to relax to the point where they touch or nearly touch the ground. For such a shooter, their thighs will rest on their flattened feet and their position will be very stable. Depending on age and physical condition, not everyone can get down this far. However, before you say you cannot do it, get down and try.

If you are a right handed shooter, your right foot should be tucked up between your left leg. The opposite is true for left handed shooters. With your legs crossed, you will now put your elbows into the natural pocket that is created by your bent legs.

We do not put our elbows on top of our knees because that creates a bone on bone situation. If you put your elbow on your knee your arm will want to roll around and you will need muscle tension to prevent that. Again, we are trying to eliminate muscle tension. There is an advanced technique for limber shooters where they flatten their legs to the ground and rest their elbows on the outside of their knees. This puts the shooter down very close to the ground and provides excellent stability.

Sitting: elbows tucked into the pocket created by the bent knees/legs.

Kneeling: The kneeling position is not as stable as the prone or sitting, but it is far more stable than standing when done correctly.

For a solid kneeling position, the support side leg is bent. The foot is placed flat on the ground and the tibia (lower leg bone) is as vertical as possible. Once more, if the tibia is pushed out or pulled in, muscle tension is required to stabilize the leg.
The dominant or shooting side knee is bent and angled at 90 degrees. The shooter sits down on their dominant side heel. How the dominant foot is

bent will again depend on the physical abilities of the shooter.

The most stable position comes from the dominant foot being flat against the ground. If the shooter cannot bend their ankle in such a way, they put the toe of their boot on the ground and sit down on the heel.

Regarding the support side elbow, again we place the elbow ahead of the knee and allow our tricep muscle to rest on it. If you cannot get your tricep on your knee, pull your elbow behind the knee and allow the carpi ulnaris (forearm muscle) to rest on the knee. What we are looking to avoid is putting the elbow on top of the knee.

The dominant or shooting arm can now relax and naturally rest beside the shooter's ribs. Cocking the shooting arm out creates muscle tension and must be avoided.

*Editor's Note: During prone, sitting, and kneeling, the palm of the support hand holds up or supports the forend of the stock. The fingers can rest loosely around the stock, but it is not necessary to have a tight grip. Too tight of a grip on the forend will add muscle tension and potential tremor to the front of the rifle.

Kneeling: support elbow in front of support knee, shooter sits on dominant heel.

Off Hand (standing): The least stable unsupported position is Off Hand as gravity is now working in full effect. Regardless, it is possible to make precise shots, even when standing unsupported. The Marine Corps teaches recruits to hit a 12 inch circle from 200 yards when standing in the Off Hand position, so it can be done it just takes effort and discipline.

Begin with the body facing 90 degrees away from the target with the support side shoulder on the target side. The feet should be spaced shoulder width apart and the weight of the body is evenly distributed between both feet. Again, leaning back or forward created muscle tension.

If you have a solid prone, sitting, or even kneeling position, it is possible to hold the muzzle of your rifle on target for a good long time, not so with Off Hand. Therefore, what we do next is critical.

With your feet evenly spaced and comfortable, place the butt of the rifle in the socket of your support side shoulder by elevating the front of the rifle above your head. When the butt is in the shoulder pocket, inhale deeply and slowly exhale. As you are exhaling, bring both of your elbows down to your rib cage. This will lower the muzzle and it will settle onto the target.

You should be in your natural respiratory pause and you will have two to three seconds to stabilize the muzzle and break the shot. The longer you hold the rifle up, the more muscle twitch you will perceive in your front sight or scope. Eventually our muzzle will be moving so much that an accurate shot becomes impossible.

If you find that you missed your window of opportunity, that is alright. Take the rifle out of your shoulder and cradle it against your body with both arms. Take a few deep, cleansing breaths and then repeat the previous steps.

There is a demon that will often pop up on the shoulder of riflemen. The demon whispers in your ear, "Just take the shot, we'll make it up later." Do not listen to that demon. He wants you to miss and then you will be angry at yourself for listening to him. It is far better to take your time and reset than to blow a shot and have to deal with the mental let down.

The good news with all of these shooting positions is that you do not need ammunition in order to master them. As a matter of fact, you should not even fire a single live round until you have practiced dry-firing dozens and potentially hundreds of times.

Going back to Parris Island. We spent an entire week dry-firing in the four basic positions (hundreds and thousands of trigger presses) before we fired a live round. The more time you spend in the positions, the more comfortable you will become with them and the more confidence you will have.

*Note: when shooting from the standing/Off Hand with a variable powered scope, turn the magnification down to the lowest setting.

Standing / Off Hand: shooter's elbows rest against ribs cage, hands close together and rifle balanced in center of the body. Feet approximately shoulder width apart.

There are no shooting benches in the field

Supports

Bipods

The most common support for a modern rifle is a folding bipod. There are numerous models on the market. I have thirty years of experience with the Harris bipods. Harris Engineering makes a variety of lengths and designs as well as adapters.

The downside of a bipod is that it adds weight to the front of your rifle. If you are carrying a rifle in the field all day, that extra weight could make a difference. As with all things in life, it's a trade off.

Magpul started producing a line of bipods a few years ago. As with all of their products, the Magpul bipod uses high-strength polymer as well as some aluminum and steel. While I do not have as much experience with the Magpul version, I have been impressed with them.

Backpacks

Many shooters would rather not put the extra weight on the front of their rifle by adding a bipod and instead will rely upon their backpack as a shooting rest when going prone.

Before GWOT[1], the USMC Sniper program did not even issue bipods. All shots were taken using field expedient rests, to include the ubiquitous ALICE[2] pack.

When I went through sniper school in 2010, I was surprised that our instructor forbade the use of bipods. For prone stability we used our Eberlestock packs. Of course, we used other field expedient objects for stability as well.

Sandbags

When we say "sandbags" what we really mean is purpose-made nylon, cloth, or leather bags filled with various materials to support our rifles. Any shooting supply outlet will likely have numerous models from which to choose.

---

[1] Global War on Terror

[2] All Purpose Light-weight Individual Carrying Equipment

Yes, if you were in a fixed position, you could use a genuine sandbag, but these will weigh 20 to 30 pounds so you are not going to carry them with you to the field.

When it comes to rifle rest bags, you will find those in the large and small variety. The large one goes under the front of the rifle and the small one is tucked up under the belly of the stock at the toe.

One trick that old school Marine snipers used to do was to pack one or two old wool socks in their packs. When they needed a rest, they would fill the sock with dirt, sand, gravel, whatever. When it was time to move they would just dump it out.

Several years back, when I was doing a lot of overland varmint hunting, I found that the added weight of a bipod was becoming an impediment. I did some analysis and realized that most of my shots were taken quickly from expedient positions and I was only using the bipod during a relatively small percentage of my shots.

I invented an object that I called the "Shooter's Redi-rest". This was a nylon shooting bag filled with relatively light weight foam. It had a strap to loop over my shoulder and in total, it weighed less than a standard Harris bipod. As an added benefit, I could use it as a pillow for all day long field outings.

Shooter working from an unusual position

Shooting Sticks

Specially designed shooting sticks come in both two and three legged configuration. These are particularly popular with hunters. The sticks are aluminum or even wood and not all that heavy.

The biggest benefit of shooting sticks is their ability to be adjusted to allow the shooter to use them from both standing, kneeling and sitting. Shooting sticks can give an advantage in the field, however, you need to practice with them. If you decide that you are going to use shooting sticks, do yourself a favor and take them to the range before you go out to hunt.

Regardless of the support you use for your rifle, keep in mind that the support should be under the forearm/forend of the rifle and not touching the barrel. Allowing the barrel to touch your support will disrupt the harmonics as the barrel flexes during the shot. This will cause an unpredictable miss.

Chapter 6

Shooters and Spotters

After the shooter has learned to master the fundamentals of marksmanship and how to operate their equipment, it is time to consider the relationship that is the "Shooter and Spotter".

Much like a spotter in the gym, a spotter on the range is there to aid and support the shooter. The shooter is responsible for making the shot, but the spotter is there to assist when assistance is needed. In the military, the spotter is the senior man and the most experienced person on the two man team. The spotter is actually the team leader.

Just as the weight lifter might fail on their attempt to push the barbell on the bench, the shooter might fail to connect with their first shot. The task of the spotter in precision shooting is to quickly offer an adjustment that will get the shooter on target. This is particularly important when the target is an unknown distance and there is wind with which to deal.

In order to be a good spotter and an effective partner, the spotter needs to be in a physical position to judge the impact of the shooter's shot.

The best position for the spotter to be in is as close to in line with the shooter's rifle as possible. One position for the spotter would be to be on the rifle side of the shooter, but behind them so as not to interfere with the operation of the rifle or to be hit by ejecting brass if such is the case.

For massive rifles, particularly .50 BMG versions, the shooter must be far enough behind the shooter so as not eat a face full of gas and debris when the rifle discharges. In such a case the spotter will be back near the shooter's legs/feet. It is possible for a spotter to call shots when lying on the off side of the shooter, but the farther the target the more difficult it will be to make a good call.

The most important aspect of the shooter/spotter relationship is that they are speaking the same language. That is, they must both be speaking and thinking in the same adjustments. For instance, if the spotter sees the bullet strike below the target and he says "Come up two." Both the shooter and spotter need to understand "two" what? Two MOA? Two Mils? Two inches or two feet? Or, does the spotter want the shooter to add two clicks of elevation? You can see how confusing this could become.

Some folks would say, "That's why everyone needs to use Mil-Dots and nothing else." Shooters and spotters can communicate in Mils, or MOA, or "clicks", as long as they are both on the same sheet of music. This is where practice and teamwork comes into play. The longer that a shooter and spotter work together, the more in tune they will be with one another.

Sometimes the terrain will dictate the location of the spotter in relation to the shooter

Spotters and shooters working together

With medium and light recoiling calibers, it is possible for the shooter to stay on target and call their shots. However, generally, the larger the caliber and the heavier the recoil, the more difficult it becomes for a shooter to spot their shots. A man shooting a .338 Lapua Magnum or even a .300 Winchester Magnum is going to find it difficult to make self-correction. Add distance and wind to the mix and a good spotter becomes invaluable.

Using a spotter is not a crutch or somehow an admission of a lack of skill. Even the great ones; Carlos Hathcock, Chuck Mawhinney, and Chris Kyle worked with spotters. Long distance riflemen who work as shooter/spotter teams are far more successful than those who do not.

Bonus Chapter

Snipers Scopes: Talking in Circles/Shooting in Straight Lines.

*Author's Note: the following was first written as an article to help folks understand Mils versus MOA and from where they both originate.

When it comes to shooting a precision rifle or sniper rifle, a great deal of your discussion will be focused (no pun intended) on the sniper scope mounted atop the gun. It should be obvious to most readers that mounting a $100 scope onto a $1000 rifle is sophomoric, a waste of valuable potential and, frankly, the sign of an amateur shooter.

Nonetheless, even experienced riflemen run into some confusion regarding which windage and elevation adjustments are the most beneficial for long range shooting or sniping. For the longest time, precision rifle scopes or sniper scopes were adjusted via a method we referred to as Minute of Angle or simply MOA. Then, some smart guy came up with the Milliradian method of scope adjustment. Before, MRAD or Mils, shooters were satisfied to calculate 1/4, 1/2, or 1 MOA adjustments. I suppose we can blame the continental Europeans or the Asians for this situation as MOA is based upon British Imperial measurement and MRAD is better translated to the Metric system (although you can still use inches when calculating Mils if your brain likes solving math problems).

Talking in Circles

Some of the confusion with both MOA and Mils is due to the fact that they are both based upon angles and degrees in a circle. For the layman, 1 MOA = 1 inch at 100 yards, 2 MOA is 2 inches at 200 yards, etc. Many people have wondered how they came up with that? Going back to "Minute of Angle", a "minute" is 1/60th of an Angle or 1 degree. There are 360 degrees on a compass or in a circle. From a technical standpoint, 1 MOA is actually 1.047 inches. Has your brain melted yet?

Milliradians are calculated by dividing the circle with which we are dealing into 6283 Mils. There are 10 Mils in 0.5625 degrees of angle. A single Mil is equal to 1/6400 of a complete circle. Sounds easy, right? One Mil or MRAD is equal to 10 centimeters or 3.6 inches at 100 yards. Unlike standard 1/4 or 1/2 inch "click" adjustments on the sniper scope knob, most of the MRAD scope adjustments are made in 0.1 Mils. Meaning ten "clicks" moves the adjustment 1 full Mil or 10 centimeters/3.6 inches at 100 yards.

Of course, all of this talk is "angular" as it is a part of a circle. But, when we shoot a rifle, the bullet path is "linear". Our brains see the image of bullets, although they spin from the rifling, going in a straight line (linear), not around in circles like the hands on a clock or the dial on a compass. The new or even old school shooter might wonder why we are talking in circles when we are shooting in straight lines?

We have not even discussed the effect of gravity on the bullet or the damnable wind that is constantly trying to blow our projectiles to the left or right. How about the effect of elevation on the flight path of the bullet? The impact of a 500 yard shot taken at sea level and a 500 yard shot taken at 7000 feet will not be the same. Then we have the magnification of error. A bullet that is 1 inch off the mark at 100 yards (or meters if that makes you happy) is not going to be 1 inch off at 300, the error is magnified on an angular scale. Shoot! Here we are talking circles again.

When you start trying to do all of these mathematical calculations in your head while sitting or lying behind a rifle, even the most seasoned shooter can feel their brain begin to hurt. Oh, in case your eyes haven't glazed over by now, every cartridge has a different velocity and every different bullet has its own unique Ballistic Coefficient that determines how well or not it flies through the atmosphere. Kind of makes you think that rifle shooting is not for dummies, huh?

Keeping it Simple

When you start to consider all of the variables, figuring out how to make consistent, one shot hits, at distances from 100 to 1000 yards or more, seems to be a daunting task. The first step is to keep it simple. The worst thing you can do for your brain is to try and work with numerous different cartridges with varied bullet designs and velocities at the same time. To do so is to set yourself up for a mental breakdown.

Rifles barrels come from the factory with varied rifling. For the .308 Winchester, the most common rifling is a 1/10 twist, but that is not an absolute. Let's say you have such a rifle. Purchase three loads of .308 ammunition, bench your rifle on sandbags or something similar and slow fire several groups onto a paper target at 100 yards. A hot barrel (several rounds fired rapidly) will group differently than a cold barrel. Take your time. If your marksmanship skills are up to par, you should know within an hour which load the rifle prefers. Yes, different rifles will shoot some loads better than others. That is simply the way of the world. (*Editor's Note: 168 and 175 grain precision ammunition in a .308 Winchester generally produce the most consistent groups, wound channels or tissue damage are a topic for another day)

Now that you have determined which load groups the most consistently from your given rifle it is time to start working on your calculations and scope adjustments. Thanks to the wonder of the internet, ballistic calculation charts for essentially every cartridge or load under the sun are at your fingertips. You can work up a rifle "dope" out to 2000 yards if you want. However, if you are limited to a 300 or 500 yard range, 1000 yard dope is just mental masturbation.

Going back to your scope adjustment, be they MOA or MRAD, you will now determine how many adjustments you will need to make to hit your target, dead center, at a given distance. A "click" is simply one adjustment of either your windage or elevation knob. It is not necessary to get all bunged up about terminology. Many years ago when I attended a Sniper School, the lead instructor explained, "For the purpose of clarity, we use the term 'clicks'. A single adjustment of the knob is a 'click' regardless of whether it is MOA or Mils." Every sniper rifle should have its own dedicated notebook. Yes, Gen Z, I mean a bound stack of paper with a protective cover. We use pencils or pens to inscribe data onto said notebook. (No, I do not care about the newest app on our iPhone.)

In the notebook we keep track of the range location (primarily the elevation of the range), the weather that day, and the critical data such as the load specifics, the zero of the rifle (most will be zeroed at 100 yds) and the number of clicks up for each target at each distance. It is one thing to work the numbers up on a ballistic calculator, it is another to actually do so in the real world. For a point of clarity, windage is set at 100 yards and we do not touch the windage knob again. Snipers do not dope (dial) wind, they use the horizontal reticle and hold over left or right depending on the direction.

To continue, when you are on target at varied distances, you will record the number of clicks. For instance, I have an M40-style rifle in .308. At two hundred yards, I will go up 2 clicks, not "half-MOA" or 0.6 Mils, just 2 clicks. At 300 yards my adjustment up is 10, (one, two, three…ten). Yes, I know some of you have spent hours upon hours studying Milliradians and now I burst your bubble. However, the point of this exercise is to keep it simple.

The ability to rapidly apply click adjustments leads us to the ability to "speed dial" our elevation knob in order to put a bullet onto a humanoid target in rapid fashion. Believe it or not, living creatures have the annoying habit of moving around and refusing to stand perfectly still while you calculate exact MOA or Mil corrections in your head. Having book knowledge or technical knowledge of Minute of Angle or Milliradian is wonderful. Nonetheless, having a great deal of practical experience behind the rifle while engaging targets at varied distances is even more useful.

The Bushnell Elite Tactical dialed to 1400 yards

Who makes the Best Sniper Scope?

There are a number of questions or assertions that are certain to instigate an argument or at very least a heated debate. "What is the best round for self-defense?" is one of these questions as is the GLOCK versus M1911 discussion. Regarding who makes the best sniper scope, again you are looking for an argument. Currently, the United States Marines Corps is using the Nightforce Optics "Advanced Tactical Scope". The United States Army, however, is going with the Leupold MkV HD riflescope. Both are excellent choices.

Old school riflemen speak of the Unertl rifle scopes with reverence, but that company no longer exists. US Optics is considered by many to be the natural successor to the Unertl reputation for rock solid,

73

crystal clear sniper scopes. Steiner Optics and Trijicon and no slouches either. Also, the precision tactical scopes from EOTech are earning a solid reputation. Bushnell has been taking tremendous steps forward with their Elite Tactical line of optics. The Brownell's MPO series is a tremendous value for a long range, fully adjustable rifle scope.

From my thirty years of shooting a precision long range rifle in the field, I can say that some of the must have features, regardless of manufacturer, would include external adjustment knobs with a positive click feel. Yes, sometimes you have to make adjustments while wearing gloves.

(*Editor's Note: I went through an entire Sniper School, to include the graduation qualification while wearing gloves. No, I did not cut off the trigger finger.)

A locking windage knob is a good feature as it does not need to be changed after zero is achieved. The parallax focus knob should also provide superior clarity and be simple to adjust. An illuminated reticle, though not an absolute, is a positive addition. Minimum tube body should be 30mm, 34mm tubes are great but not a requirement. Variable power is nice, but once more not critical.

I have been on the range with a shooter using a US Army fixed 10x rifle scope and watched as he smacked a steel target at 1000 yards. The US Army sniper scope in WWII was a fixed 8x. In Vietnam, the USMC used a fixed 8x Unertl riflescope. Carlos Hathcock recorded ninety-three confirmed kills in Vietnam with a fixed power scope.

Additionally, while the "bigger the better" might seem to be the obvious solution, there are downsides to high magnification rifle scopes, particularly when you start getting into powers higher than 10x or 12x. High magnification will increase the perceived movement of the reticle. The higher you dial the scope, the more important absolute stability becomes. Depending on your setup, "concrete shooting bench" stability might not be possible. Also, high magnification magnifies the atmospheric mirage that is a combination of sunlight and humidity. If all you can see through your scope is waves, you need to turn down the magnification.Fixed power scopes can get the job done.

A scope shade or type of "kill flash" filter affixed to the objective lens should also be on your shopping list.

Notice that I did not say you absolutely have to use MOA or MRAD. MRAD adjustments with Mil-Dot reticles certainly do offer advantages, I will not argue with that. Nonetheless, it is the man who shoots the rifle, not the scope. We cannot replace skill and experience with equipment. Gear enhances skill, not the other way around. The bottomline is to figure out what load is the most consistent in your chosen rifle and spend as much time as you can behind that gun.

The author working as a Small Arms & Tactics Instructor for the US Military

Author SME/Instructor Vitae

Paul G. Markel has worn many hats during his lifetime. He has been a U.S. Marine, Police Officer, Professional Bodyguard, and Small Arms and Tactics Instructor.

Mr. Markel is an Amazon #1 Best-selling Author with numerous books in print. Paul has been writing professionally for law enforcement, outdoors, and firearms periodicals for thirty plus years with hundreds upon hundreds of articles in print.

Paul Markel is the creator of all Student of the Gun media ventures. His duties include writing, hosting, and producing Student of the Gun TV and Radio, as well as innumerable written works found on StudentoftheGun.com.

Markel has also contributed to The Blaze and been a guest host of other nationally syndicated radio shows.

Mr. Markel's professional education includes:

- Executive Security International
  - Executive Protection and Bodyguard studies
  - Intelligence Gathering and Investigation
  - Advanced Firearms training under John S. Farnam

- **United States Marine Corps** service training *Combat Decorated Veteran*
  - Basic Training: Physical Fitness, Rifle Marksmanship, Swim Qualification, First Aid, Marine Corps History and Traditions
  - School of the Infantry: Anti-Tank Assault, Patrolling, Ambush Techniques, Nighttime and Low Light Operations

- Sea Service Indoctrination School: Shipboard Firefighting and Damage Control, Naval Service traditions, Advanced Physical Training, Advanced Marksmanship Training, Customs and Courtesies
  - Shipboard Security Engagement Training (SSET) and Nuclear Weapons Storage and Security School, Fast Reaction Team training
  - Demolitions, Mines and Explosive Ordnance School
  - USMC Marksmanship Coaches School
  - Desert Survival Training
  - Jungle Warfare Indoctrination and Patrolling
  - USMC Leadership Training / NCO Course

- Ohio State Peace Officers Academy (State Police Academy)

- Special Weapons and Tactics Manual Structure Breaching School

- Advanced Firearms Training Courses
  - Gunsite Academy: Rifle, Pistol, Shotgun courses

- - Tactical Defense Institute: Close Quarters Fighting, Pistol, and Rifle courses
  - SIG Academy: Pistol, Carbine, Shotgun, Long Range Rifle courses
  - Tactical Response: Fighting Pistol and Fighting Rifle, Close Quarters Fighting courses, Fight Strong Strength Training
  - Ken Hackathorn: Advanced Handgun and Carbine Course
  - International Tactical Training Systems: Urban Sniper School
  - Blackwater Academy: Advanced Shotgun course
  - Expeditionary Combat Skills: Advanced Rifle and Pistol, Tactical Combat Casualty Care, Judgment-based Engagement Training

- Instructor Courses
  - SureFire Academy: Low Light Tactics Instructor School
  - U.S.M.C. Marksmanship Coaches School
  - U.S. Navy Marksmanship Coaches School
  - Tidewater Community College Instructor Training Course

- o Oleoresin Capsicum Aerosol Training Instructor Trainer School
- o Red Cross CPR and Family First Aid Instructor course
- o National Rifle Association: Handgun, Rifle, and Shotgun Instructor School, Range Safety Officers School,
- o NRA Law Enforcement Handgun and Shotgun Instructor school
- o National 4H Youth Firearms Instructors School

Mr. Markel has been teaching safe and effective firearms handling to students young and old for decades and has worked actively with the 4-H Shooting Sports program. Paul holds numerous instructor certifications in multiple disciplines; nonetheless, he is and will remain a dedicated Student of the Gun.

Other Books from Paul G. Markel

Patriot Fire Team Manual

Patriot Fire Team Equipment Guide

Examining the Armed Citizen

SOTG Instructor Development Manual

www.ingramcontent.com/pod-product-compliance
Lightning Source LLC
Chambersburg PA
CBHW071945120726
48001CB00005B/2047